Chimpanzees

Chimpanzees

Mary Ann McDonald

T H E   C H I L D ' S   W O R L D®, INC.

Library of Congress Cataloging-in-Publication Data
McDonald, Mary Ann.
Chimpanzees / by Mary Ann McDonald.
p.   cm.
Includes index.
Summary: Describes the physical characteristics,
behavior, habitat, and life cycle of the chimpanzee.
ISBN 1-56766-497-0 (lib. bdg. : alk paper)
1. Chimpanzees—Juvenile literature.
[1. Chimpanzees.]   I. Title.
QL737.P96M425   1998
599.885—dc21   97-44646
CIP
AC

Photo Credits

© 1996 Anup Shah/Dembinsky Photo Assoc. Inc: cover
© 1997 Anup Shah/Dembinsky Photo Assoc. Inc: 10, 19
© Connie Bransilver: 13
© Joe McDonald: 9, 15, 20
© Mary Ann McDonald: 16
© Robert and Linda Mitchell: 2, 6, 30
© 1996 Stan Osolinski/Dembinsky Photo Assoc. Inc: 23
© 1997 Stan Osolinski/Dembinsky Photo Assoc. Inc: 24, 26, 29

On the cover...

Front cover: This chimpanzee lives in Africa.
Page 2: This young chimpanzee is chewing on a plant.

Table of Contents

Meet the Chimpanzee!

As you walk through a steamy jungle, you hear a strange noise high in the trees. "AH-HUA UAH-UAH UAH!!!" You look up and see a large animal sitting on a branch. It scratches its head and calls out again. What could this creature be? It's our closest relative in the animal world—the chimpanzee.

What Are Chimpanzees?

Chimpanzees belong to a group of animals called **primates**. Apes, monkeys, and people are primates, too. Primates are different from other animals in the way they think, communicate with each other, and use their hands and feet.

Chimpanzees belong to the **great apes**, a group of primates that includes orangutans, gibbons, and gorillas. Chimpanzees are very smart. In fact, they are considered the most intelligent of the great apes.

This chimpanzee is eating a midday snack. ⇒

What Do Chimpanzees Look Like?

Chimpanzees are the smallest of the great apes, but they are still fairly large—about 5 feet tall. They have large ears and dark eyes. They have strong arms and legs, too. Male chimpanzees have very long, sharp teeth.

Fur covers most of a chimpanzee's body. In fact, the only places without fur are the chimpanzee's face, the palms of its hands, and the bottoms of its feet. The fur is very thick and is often black or brown.

⇐ This young chimpanzee is hanging on a vine.

Where Do Chimpanzees Live?

Chimpanzees live only in the warm areas of Africa. There they live in rain forests, grassy woodlands, and other forests. Sadly, many of the places chimpanzees live are being destroyed to make way for farms, houses, and cities.

Chimpanzees are **arboreal**, which means that they spend most of their lives in the trees. Trees are important sources of food for chimpanzees. They are also a safe place where the chimpanzees can rest during the day and sleep at night.

This adult chimpanzee is resting on some branches. ⇒

Why do chimpanzees live in trees? Because trees keep them safe from animals that might hunt and eat them. These meat-eating animals are called **predators**. *Leopards* are one kind of predator that eats chimpanzees.

The chimpanzees escape from predators by climbing high in the trees. They grasp branches with their hands and feet, moving through the treetops quickly and easily.

Chimpanzees like this one are safe in the trees. ⇒

How Do Chimpanzees Sleep?

Like people, chimpanzees are **diurnal**, which means that they are active during the daytime and sleep at night. They eat mainly in the morning and late afternoon. During the middle of the day, they like to take a nap.

At night, each chimpanzee finds a forked tree or some crossed branches and builds a cozy nest. The chimp bends or breaks some strong branches and makes a comfortable place to sleep. Holding each branch with its feet, the chimpanzee weaves it over and under the other branches. Leaves make the bed soft and keep the chimpanzee warm.

← This mother and baby chimpanzee are taking an afternoon nap.

Do Chimpanzees Live in Groups?

Chimpanzees travel and **forage**, or look for food, alone or in small groups. Females travel with their young and sometimes with other females. Males usually join small groups. Groups that get along well make up a chimpanzee community. A chimp community might have up to 120 animals living in it! The community never gathers together all at the same time, but all the animals know each other. The community stakes out an area that the males defend against outsiders.

These young chimpanzees live together in a group. ⇒

Male chimpanzees spend their entire lives in the communities where they were born. Females, though, must leave their community when they become adults. They must find a new community that will accept them. The females face many dangers as they search for new homes.

What Are Baby Chimpanzees Like?

Female chimpanzees usually have their first baby when they are about 12 years old. They protect the baby, clean it, and give it food. In fact, milk from its mother's body is a baby chimpanzee's most important food until it is two years old.

By the time it is 6 months old, the baby starts to walk, ride on its mother's back, and nibble on food. When it is about 8 years old, the young chimpanzee becomes independent. At that age, the young females leave to find their new communities. The young males stay close to their mothers, but live their own lives.

This baby chimpanzee is holding on to its mother. ⇒

How Do Chimpanzees Communicate?

Just like us, chimpanzees touch each other, make sounds, and make faces and signals. And just like us, a chimpanzee's face can show anger, fear, or happiness. Mothers chimpanzees often kiss and hug their youngsters. Adults reach out and touch each other with their hands. Chimpanzees groom each other, too. When they are angry, chimpanzees charge at each other, wave their arms, throw things, stamp their feet, or swing from branches.

⇐ Chimpanzees like this one can show their feelings with their faces.

Chimpanzees make more sounds than any other animal. They whine when they are hurt or lonely. When they are angry, they cry out loudly. They squeak, scream, grunt, and bark at other times. Chimpanzees use one call, called the *pant-hoot*, when they are very excited. They make this sound when they want to call others far away. Chimpanzees make this loud sound by shaping their lips into a trumpet and breathing out hard.

What Do Chimpanzees Eat?

Chimpanzees eat mainly fruit. They also eat young leaves, bark, flowers, and tree sap. Insects are an important food at certain times, too. Chimpanzees eat termites, ants, caterpillars, and even insect eggs. They also hunt small animals when they have the chance. Male chimpanzees sometimes hunt and kill monkeys, baby birds, small antelopes, and other animals.

This chimpanzee is munching on large leaves. ⇒

Do Chimpanzees Use Tools?

Chimpanzees are the only apes known to use tools in the wild. They use grass and sticks to "fish" for insects called *termites* that live in huge mounds. They soak up water and clean their fur with "sponges" made of chewed or wadded-up leaves. And they use rocks or wooden clubs to crack open nuts or other foods that have shells.

Chimpanzees are smart, fun-loving animals. So the next time you see a chimpanzee acting in a movie, remember that it's not just a dumb animal. It knows what it is doing! If we work to protect the chimpanzees and the forests they call home, these fascinating animals will be with us for a long, long time.

← Chimpanzees like this one are very smart.

Glossary

arboreal (ar–BOR–ee–ull)
An arboreal animal spends most of its life in the trees. Chimpanzees are mostly arboreal.

diurnal (die–UR–null)
A diurnal animal is active during the daytime and sleeps at night. People are diurnal, and so are chimpanzees.

forage (FOR–edge)
Foraging is looking for food. Chimpanzees forage by themselves or in small groups.

great apes (GRATE APES)
Great apes is a name for certain kinds of primates—chimpanzees, gibbons, orangutans, and gorillas. The great apes are highly intelligent.

predators (PREH–deh–terz)
Predators are animals that hunt and kill other animals. Leopards are one kind of predator that hunts and eats chimpanzees.

primates (PRY–mates)
Primates are an animal family that includes apes, monkeys, and people. Primates think and use their hands and feet differently from other animals.

Index